The Walter Lynwood Fleming
Lectures in Southern History

Louisiana State University

Other Published Lectures in This Series

The Repressible Conflict, 1830–1861   AVERY O. CRAVEN

Three Virginia Frontiers   THOMAS PERKINS ABERNETHY

South America and Hemisphere Defense   J. FRED RIPPY

The Plain People of the Confederacy   BELL IRVIN WILEY

Behind the Lines in the Southern Confederacy
CHARLES W. RAMSDELL

Lincoln and the South   J. G. RANDALL

The Rural Press and the New South   THOMAS D. CLARK

Plain Folk of the Old South   FRANK LAWRENCE OWSLEY

Confederate Leaders in the New South   WILLIAM B. HESSELTINE

The Texas Revolution   WILLIAM C. BINKLEY

Myths and Realities   CARL BRIDENBAUGH

The South Lives in History   WENDELL HOLMES STEPHENSON

Civil War in the Making, 1815–1860   AVERY O. CRAVEN

The Fall of Richmond   REMBERT W. PATRICK

The First South   JOHN RICHARD ALDEN

The Mind of the Old South   CLEMENT EATON

F.D.R. and the South   FRANK FREIDEL

Religious Strife on the Southern Frontier
WALTER BROWNLOW POSEY

The Politics of Reconstruction, 1863–1867   DAVID DONALD

Three Carpetbag Governors   RICHARD N. CURRENT

The Slave Power Conspiracy and the Paranoid Style
DAVID BRION DAVIS

THE SOUTH
AND THE
CONCURRENT
MAJORITY

DAVID M. POTTER

THE SOUTH
AND THE
CONCURRENT
MAJORITY

EDITED BY
DON E. FEHRENBACHER
AND
CARL N. DEGLER

LOUISIANA STATE UNIVERSITY PRESS/BATON ROUGE

ISBN 0-8071-0229-6
Library of Congress Catalog Card Number 72–84123
Copyright © 1972 by Louisiana State University Press
All rights reserved
Manufactured in the United States of America
Printed by Vail-Ballou Press, Inc.,
Binghamton, New York
Designed by Albert R. Crochet

Preface

𝒟 AVID M. POTTER delivered these Walter Lynwood Fleming Lectures at Louisiana State University on April 22 and 23, 1968. Thereafter other commitments and duties intervened, and at the time of his death on February 18, 1971, he had scarcely begun the work of preparing the lectures for publication. The first lecture, we discovered, was typewritten and so had presumably undergone some revision; the other two were still in their original handwritten form, characteristically looking like very rough draft but reading like final draft, virtually ready for the printer. One reading was enough to convince us that the essays should be published; and such was our recommendation to David Potter's daughter and heir, Catherine Potter, and to the Louisiana State University Press. They are presented without apology and need none: yet it should be remembered that the essays are probably not quite as Potter himself would have published them, for they lack not only his final literary polish, but also the afterthoughts that no doubt would have come to him with further reflection on his subject.

Certain costs of preparing the lectures for publication have been defrayed by the Institute of American History at Stanford University, and we are grateful also for typing assistance to several members of the secretarial staff in the Stanford Department of History. The editors thought it advisable to secure a thorough check of the numerous statistics with which Potter reinforced his generalizations about Southern influence in national politics. This work of verification was performed by two graduate students in history at Stanford University, Mark A. Paul and Michel R. Dahlin. Corrections resulting from their careful investigations have necessitated some changes in the text, and we have also made some minor stylistic revisions. For the most part, however, these are very much the same lectures that David M. Potter delivered to an appreciative audience some four years ago.

Don E. Fehrenbacher
Carl N. Degler
Stanford, California
April, 1972

Contents

Preface   vii

1   The Concurrent Majority: Rejected in
    Theory, Accepted in Practice   3

2   The Political Parity of a Minority Section   29

3   Rearguard Actions on the Southern Retreat   61

THE SOUTH
AND THE
CONCURRENT
MAJORITY

1

The Concurrent Majority:
Rejected in Theory
Accepted in Practice

*T*HE basic theme of this volume is a consideration of the political devices by which, for nearly a hundred years, the South has contrived to maintain a position of power in the national government and a position in which it could maintain its basic sectional objectives despite adverse majorities in the nation. That position of power is rapidly crumbling today; but historically the remarkable fact is that, for a century and a half after the South began to pass perceptibly into a minority position in terms of population and for a century after it suffered smashing defeat in the Civil War, the region still was able to maintain an entrenched position in the American political system from which it could fight on equal terms against political adversaries who outnumbered it more than three to one. James MacGregor Burns, in his *The Deadlock of Democracy,* has remarked:

"If a test of political expertness is the capacity to convert limited political resources into maximum governmental power, the most expert of the politicians in Washington today are the leaders of the congressional Democratic party." These leaders are still preponderantly Southern leaders, and it is the Southern wing of the party to which Burns is alluding when he goes on to say: "They represent a tiny fraction of the nation's electorate; the approximately 90 members of this party in the House are elected by about two million of the nation's sixty million voters. Those 90 members make up less than one-fourth of the House [which has a total of 435 members]; they cannot by themselves muster enough votes even for a veto when a two-thirds vote is required. But they make up for their lack of numbers in the quality of their political craftsmanship, their grasp of the relation of policy goals and political means, and of course their control of congressional machinery."

John C. Calhoun, on his deathbed, is supposed to have exclaimed unhappily, "The South, the poor South, what will become of her!" No one can say what he might think had become of the South if he could revisit it in 1968. No doubt the open housing law adopted earlier this month would seem to him the ultimate defeat of the South as he conceived it. Carthage, he might say, has been destroyed. But if he could see the power wielded by the "congressional Democratic party" of which Burns speaks, he would

4

current majority. Without this there can be no negative, and without a negative, no constitution.''

Abstract and powerful political thinker that he
was, Calhoun recognized that any functionally negative power exercised by a section (the South) would
contribute to a system whereby decisions were made
jointly by the minority and the majority, and not by
the majority alone. He recognized that this power
might take any of several forms—''be it called by
what term it may.'' Recognizing this, he probably
would recognize that the system of control of committee chairmanship through which the South has
entrenched itself at the crucial loci of power in Congress—the system of seniority, and the historical
tactic of the South in controlling the government
through its control of the Democratic Party, as well
as the two-thirds rule in party conventions prior to
1936, and the use of the filibuster in the Senate—that
all of these devices are instrumentalities of the concurrent majority. But if he had recognized it, he
would have done so with some astonishment, for although he recognized functional devices, he was at
heart a formalist and preferred formal institutional
modes of sectional self-defense. Hence he thought in
terms of a doctrine of state sovereignty, a doctrine
of the right of state interposition against or nullification of federal laws, and a doctrine of secession.
His clearest proposal for the concurrent majority,
set forth in the *Discourse on the Constitution,* was

for a dual executive—two Presidents, one Northern
and one Southern—each with a right of veto. This
was perhaps the most theoretical of all his fine-spun
formulations, and also the least influential. But it
has significance because it illustrates his fondness
for formal constructs: What could be more formal
than to adopt a double presidency for the United
States like the dual consulship of ancient Rome? It
illustrates, too, his speculative fondness for theory
and his tendency to embrace an entirely impracticable theory as readily as he would a theory which
might have some chance of being put into operation.

Of course, as his present-day critics point out, his
theory was not really broad enough to defend all
minority rights—he was the defender of the vested
interests of one section in particular rather than of
minorities in general, and he was utterly oblivious to
the minority interest of the slaves. Critics might also
point out that his theory was perhaps unduly abstract, in the sense that he was prone to value proposed techniques of minority defense for their logical
elegance rather than for their operative practicality.
Thus it is paradoxical that he stated the essence of
the program which the South was successfully to
adopt and maintain for nearly a century after his
death, namely, to gain and hold a point at which negative power could be exercised. But he misconceived
almost completely the context in which the South
was to accomplish its sectional purpose. He stated a

theory, which was to be implemented by nullification, or secession, or a dual presidency. He rejected the practicalities of party politics, regarded party affiliation as an impediment to loyalty to the South, and urged that the South unite in an exclusively sectional bloc to attain its objectives. By the irony of history, the South accepted his theory that negative power must be attained and held, but it rejected the means which he proposed and adopted the means which he rejected. Because his cherished and highly articulated plans for nullification, joint action by the Southern states in a Southern convention, and a dual executive have long since gone into the dustbin of obsolete historical ideas, he has been left with a reputation as a sterile although wonderfully ingenious political metaphysician and spokesman of lost causes. Because his means were rejected, even the South, which followed the essence of his theory and found its ways to exercise a negative through the very institution which he regarded as least promising, namely, the political party, even the South failed to recognize that Calhoun's theory was not obsolete but was in fact very much alive. It likewise failed to recognize that the theory was to guide Southern political behavior for more than a century after Calhoun's death and that the principle of the concurrent majority, far from being a metaphysical abstraction, had been one of the dominant facts of American political life throughout most of our history.

The conditions which ultimately enabled the South to exercise a concurrent majority lay in two things: first, the organizational and procedural structure of the American Congress; and second, the peculiar circumstances of the Democratic Party which rendered it subject to Southern control.

The Congress, at the time when Calhoun wrote his *Disquisition,* had already been in operation for about sixty years. When it first met, no one envisioned a system of legislative committees. But from the outset, it proved impracticable to act upon proposed legislation on the floor without some preliminary consideration, and therefore *ad hoc* committees were created to study and report upon each important bill as it was presented. However, as soon as the volume of proposed legislation reached any appreciable size, the number of committees became excessive. There were, for instance, about three hundred fifty separate *ad hoc* committees in the Third Congress, 1793–1795. But this was an intolerable number, and first the House and then the Senate began to establish standing committees. In 1800 the House had four standing committees; by 1810, nine; and by 1816, thirteen. The Senate, which was a very small body in its early days, developed its standing committees more slowly and had as many as ninety select or *ad hoc* committees as late as 1816. Until that year it had only four standing committees, two of which were joint with the House. But in 1816 it turned decisively to the system of standing committees, creating eleven such instruments at one time. From 1816 on, then, both houses of Congress were committed to vesting important responsibilities in their committees. By 1822 the House adopted a rule that "the several standing committees of the House shall have leave to report any bill or otherwise." As Congress adopted the practice of referring each measure of proposed legislation to a standing committee, it in effect gave the committees important powers, and especially important negative powers to obstruct legislation which the committee did not approve. In the early practice of the House, a bill could be taken from an obstructive committee by the passage of a motion to discharge the committee, and it is said that for a short time the practice of discharge was frequent but that it was discontinued at an early date. By 1867 a motion to discharge a committee had ceased to be privileged, and for the remainder of the century it was virtually impossible to bring a bill to the floor without favorable committee action.

If the power of the full Senate and the full House was limited on the one hand by their own committees, it was limited on the other by the party caucus. The division by which everyone active in public life became either a Federalist or an anti-Federalist, of course, took place very early; and by the first half of Washington's second term, the Federalists, and especially the Federalist senators, were said to meet

cies by which Thomas Jefferson coordinated the executive and legislative branches of the government and, in effect, imposed the executive policy. As John Marshall expressed it, Jefferson sought "to embody himself with the House." At first he was highly successful in doing so. With Albert Gallatin acting as a kind of intermediary between the President and Congress, and often entertaining congressmen at his house in meetings which were in effect caucuses; with Nathaniel Macon, a trusted lieutenant, in the Speaker's chair appointing staunch Jeffersonians to the committee chairmanships; with Jefferson in regular consultation with congressional leaders; and with John Randolph, another administration stalwart, at the head of the crucial committee on Ways and Means, the committee system and the caucus operated as devices of executive control more than as instrumentalities of an autonomous Congress.

But as James MacGregor Burns has so ably shown, there is a strong tendency toward divergence between the "congressional party" and the "presidential party" in the American political system, and this divergence began to make itself felt even before Jefferson left office. As Jefferson moved toward a stronger application of federal power, some of the fundamentalist Jeffersonians, including Macon and Randolph, turned against him. Having once installed them in positions of congressional power, Jefferson could not readily uproot them, and he found himself obliged to leave Macon in the Speakership. But a threat in the House to deprive the Speaker of the power to name committees, although unsuccessful, was enough to induce Macon in 1805 to replace Randolph with Joseph Clay of Pennsylvania on Ways and Means. In 1807 the administration forces took the Speakership from Macon and gave it to Joseph Varnum of Massachusetts.

Clearly the inviolability of seniority had not yet been established, and the Congress was not yet autonomous. But this was in fact almost the last time that an American President could intervene freely in the power structure of Congress. Under Madison the congressional party became increasingly restless, and when the War Hawks came into the House in 1811, they elected a freshman congressman and a critic of the administration, Henry Clay of Kentucky, as their speaker. Incidentally, John C. Calhoun was a participant in this operation.

Soon it appeared that instead of the President controlling Congress, Congress would control the presidency, for the congressional caucus began to choose party nominees for the presidency. In fact the party caucuses had "nominated" Jefferson and Adams in 1800, but that nomination was in the nature of a ratification of a party decision already made. By 1808, however, the caucus was asserting a primary voice in the selection of party candidates for the presidency. As the nominating role of the caucus expanded, it also excited increasing popular criticism, until the adherents of Andrew Jackson introduced a new nominating device, the party convention. When the first Democratic convention assembled in 1832, the system of representation by a fixed number of delegates proportioned to the representation in the electoral college had not yet been fully established, and neither Alabama nor South Carolina was represented. Some states were clearly overrepresented in the convention and others clearly underrepresented; and to avoid a nomination in which the overrepresented delegations might exercise a disproportionate voice, the convention adopted a rule that the vote of two-thirds of the delegates would be required to make a nomination.

The rise of the nominating convention marked the fact that the party caucus had passed its high-water mark. Thereafter the caucus fell back from its intervention in presidential politics, and as the rivalry between Whigs and Democrats replaced that between Federalists and Jeffersonians, rank-and-file congressmen proved increasingly reluctant to be bound by caucus decisions on questions of legislative policy. They resisted the arrangement by which their party would tell them how to vote on a given bill, for American congressmen have always been more oriented to their constituents than to their national party organization. As the slavery contest began to wax warm in the 1830s, it became acutely evident that no party management would dare to try to tell Northern Whigs or Democrats to support a proslavery measure, or Southern Whigs or Democrats to support an antislavery one. Accordingly the range of activities covered by the party caucus became very much restricted and dwindled almost to a single question—but one which was very important—this was the question of organization of the Senate and the House. In these bodies, by the time of Andrew Jackson, both the processes of legislation and the intricacies of parliamentary procedure had grown so complex and the resources for obstruction had grown so extensive, that no effective action could take place unless approval was attained from certain strategic figures: from the committee chairmen, without whose consent the committee to which a bill was referred might never meet; from the committee on rules, in the House, for without a priority from this committee, even a bill favorably reported by a standing committee might never be brought to the floor; and from the Speaker of the House or the president *pro tempore* of the Senate, whose decision whether to nod to Congressman A or to Congressman B, both clamoring for recognition, might determine the course of legislative procedure for days to come. In short there had grown up in both Senate and House a party organization, and the caucus was sometimes the servant and sometimes master of the organization. The members of the majority party in caucus determined who would be the Speaker and who would be the president *pro tempore*. They elected the floor leaders. At some times they have controlled committee appointments directly by caucus vote or caucus approval of the recommendations of a caucus committee, or by delegating this power to the Speaker whom they have elected. Beginning in 1791, the year of the Second Congress, the Speaker had named the committees, or later had named members to fill committee vacancies. In the Senate, for the first half century, committees were named sometimes by ballot, sometimes by the president *pro tempore,* sometimes by the Vice-President. The system of selecting the committees' chairmen was not at all rigid, and at times even a distinguished member of the minority party was sometimes permitted to retain a chairmanship. The chairmanship of a Senate committee might go to the member who had received the highest vote in the balloting, or it might be determined by balloting within the committee. But when the first Congress of the Polk administration assembled, the lines were drawn far tighter, the control of the caucus as contrasted with the Senate or House as a whole was strengthened; and at the same time the caucus accepted a new and self-imposed criterion which limited the latitude of its own choice—the criterion of seniority as the basis for selecting the chairman. The development took place quite perceptibly, for there was an open fight over whether

Vice-President George M. Dallas should name the committees, and Dallas himself argued that members on the committee should rank according to the number of ballots they had received. But Senator Ambrose Sevier of Arkansas proposed instead to place majority members first and to rank them in a different order which was in fact based upon the length of their service. Thirteen days after the controversy began, and after two committees had been selected by ballot, the Senate suddenly agreed by unanimous consent to accept a list of Democratic members from Senator Sevier and a list of Whig members from Senator Jesse Speight. Both lists were ranked in order of length of service.

A wonderful device to eliminate friction had been evolved. Interparty friction was banished by an arrangement in which each party named an agreed number of members to each committee. Intraparty friction was banished by letting seniority of service on the committee determine the chairmanship automatically, and by never dropping anyone from a committee except a low-ranking member whose party representation had to be reduced because it had passed from the majority into the minority. And friction within the ranks of one party was shielded from the gaze of the other by confirming all the choices of new members whose names were added at the foot of the rank—by making and confirming these choices not in the presence of newspaper reporters and with political adversaries looking on, but in the privacy of a closed party caucus.

At the next Congress, the same procedure was followed, and Senator John P. Hale of New Hampshire, a Free Soiler and neither a Whig nor a Democrat, protested angrily that he "wanted it to appear in the record that this thing [the slate of committees] was arranged by a Democratic caucus, that the committees were fixed there, and now the motion is that we register the decrees of the caucus." Totally unperturbed by this cry of outrage, Senator Lewis Cass replied, "That is it, exactly."

Thus, by 1848 the power of the committee system had been established; the importance of long-continued service or seniority as the path to the powerful committee chairmanships had been fixed; and the ascendancy of the caucus had been confirmed as a means of controlling the organization indirectly through control of the Speakership, the selection of floor leaders, and the appointment of new members to committees.

Now, what, you may ask, has all this to do with the concurrent majority? Calhoun knew about all these things, but he did not regard them as applicable to the concurrent majority. He knew also that the Southern Democrats had used the two-thirds rule to prevent Martin Van Buren from gaining the Democratic nomination, even after Van Buren had at-

the North and divided the South about equally with his opponents; * in 1840 William Henry Harrison, turning the tables, won a bisectional victory; in 1844 James K. Polk turned the tables again and likewise won electoral majorities in both the North and the South. In 1848 the Louisiana slaveholder Zachary Taylor, with the help of such antislavery Whigs as Abraham Lincoln and William H. Seward, carried an electoral majority in the free states as well as in his native South. In 1852 Franklin Pierce won all but two of the slave states and all but two of the free states on a platform proclaiming the finality of the Compromise of 1850. This was the twelfth presidential election in the history of the republic, and, more often than not, the winners of these twelve elections had carried an electoral majority of the slave states and of the free states. No one in 1852 could have dreamed that the next time both the South and the non-South would give the preponderance of their electoral vote to the same candidate, it would be to a man who was still unborn in 1852. Woodrow Wilson would achieve such a victory in 1912, but even then he would not win a majority of the popular vote outside the South. Not until nineteen presidential elections had passed and there was another candidate named Franklin—Franklin Roosevelt in 1932—would

* In the thirteen slave states, Van Buren, 61; Whigs, 54; other candidates, 11 (South Carolina). The popular vote in twelve states (South Carolina had none) was: Van Buren, 212,693; Whig candidates (Harrison and White), 212,936.

any candidate win with victories based upon popular majorities in both sections, as victorious candidates had customarily done during the first decades of the republic.

Franklin Pierce in fact failed to carry a clear popular majority in the free states, for the combined Whig and Free Soil vote in those states slightly exceeded his. But his victory was a true bisectional one, for he carried with him into office a top-heavy majority of Democratic congressmen, including 91 free state and 67 slave state members. This was a formidable and politically valuable combination, capable of exercising immense power. Each wing of the party was strong—apparently strong enough to command the respect of the other and to insist that any important party action should be based upon a bisectional consensus. Sectional equilibrium thus seemed assured.

But all these prospects were shattered, and the destiny of the Democratic Party was altered for nearly a century to come, when Stephen A. Douglas secured the support of the President, at the beginning of Pierce's first Congress, for making the Kansas-Nebraska Act an administration measure. There is neither time nor necessity for me to go today into the troubled question of what impelled Douglas to stake his future on the repeal of the Missouri Compromise. That is a complex and speculative subject. But there is nothing complex or speculative about the effect of repeal upon the Northern wing of the congressional Democratic party. It almost destroyed it. Many of the Northern Democrats, deeply offended by the repeal itself and also by the whiphand tactics of Douglas in the Senate and of Alexander Stephens in the South, withdrew from the party. Many others, who voted reluctantly for the repeal, under the immense pressures of party regularity, were defeated at the polls in the following November.

In the elections of 1854, Northern Democratic representation in the House fell at one stroke from 91 to 25, while Southern representation slipped only slightly, from 67 to 58. Southern Democrats now outnumbered Northern Democrats more than two to one.

This meant that after 1854 the Southern wing could dominate the party organization in Congress as it had never been able to do before. Except for an interlude during the Civil War and Reconstruction, the Northern Democrats never again reached parity with the Southern Democrats in the House until the days of the New Deal, and for much of the time they were a small minority. In 1856 they rallied from their crushing post-Nebraska defeat, capturing 53 free state seats instead of 25, but in the councils of the party they were still outnumbered by 75 Southerners, and in the Senate the Southern wing of the party outweighed them 25 to 12. In 1858 their strength

22

purpose after he enunciated his Freeport Doctrine, during the Lincoln-Douglas debates. Thus, when the short session of the Thirty-fifth Congress met in December, 1858, the Democratic caucus in the Senate took up the question of Douglas' chairmanship of the Committee on Territories—an important post which he had held for eleven years. The Democratic caucus had a committee on committees, and its chairman, William M. Gwin, a senator from California but a native of Tennessee, brought to the caucus a motion to displace Douglas from his leadership in the Committee on Territories. His motion was reported to have passed in the caucus by a vote of 17–7. This probably could not have happened if Southern Democratic senators had not outnumbered their Northern fellow Democrats by 25 to 12. This action, of course, caused great bitterness among Northern Democrats and led to some discussion on the Senate floor of the committee system as a whole. In the course of this discussion, Senator George E. Pugh, looking hard at his Southern associates, commented incisively on the advantage which the seniority system had already given to the South. "You say," he asserted, "you have a usage in the Senate, first, never to displace a Senator from a Committee without his own consent and second, never to promote anyone over him. . . . Your usage is intolerably bad. . . . It has operated to give Senators from slave-holding states the chairmanship of every single committee

eleven scattered delegates, Douglas actually reached the majority on total of 152 votes on the thirty-second ballot, and held it through the thirty-fifth. Without the two-thirds rule, or in other words in any convention except the Democratic, he could have been nominated on a perfectly regular basis even though six states had walked out. With the two-thirds rule, his opponents could have defeated him without going so far as to walk out. The disruption of the Charleston convention in 1860 and the second disruption which took place when the convention reassembled at Baltimore were indicative of the fact that divisive elements in the South no longer felt safe with a concurrent majority built merely upon dominance within one of the two political parties, and they were gravitating toward the final act of secession. In their impatience they broke up the Democratic Party when almost certainly they might have prevented the nomination of Douglas without breaking it up. The fact that they did this suggests that they did not fully appreciate the degree to which they were still able to exercise what Calhoun had called a veto, the essential feature of a concurrent voice. But for six years, their dominance in the Democratic Party had given them such a concurrent voice; and in 1856 it had enabled them to elect James Buchanan to the presidency, although he carried only four free states in the election. These Southerners often paid their tribute to the memory of Calhoun, but when they did so

26

they did not mention the concurrent voice. The devices of party control may have seemed too flimsy or too lacking in the formalistic structure which Calhoun's theory stressed. Yet he had spoken of "preventing or arresting the action of the government . . . in all its forms and under all names." Certainly it is arguable that the power of the caucus, the control of committee chairmanships, and the potency of seniority were forms for arresting the action of the majority; and if this is true, it is also arguable that while the South had forgotten Calhoun's fanciful and vagrant idea of a dual executive—had in a sense rejected the concurrent majority in theory—it had for at least six years adopted the concurrent majority in practice by means of its peculiarly entrenched position in the Democratic Party.

In 1861, after Lincoln had been elected in a campaign in which he carried all of the free states except part of New Jersey, and not one of the slave states, the Southerners tried another of Calhoun's remedies —the remedy of secession. In doing so they abandoned the advantages of their favored place in the Democratic Party, and for almost a decade the Northern Democrats had to go it alone, which they could not do very successfully. But as we all know, secession was not successful either. After four years of war, the Southern states were hauled involuntarily back into the Union. As they returned the political questions reverted to the ones which Calhoun had known. How could the South protect its interests, or what it believed to be its interests, as a minority section within the Union? Was a concurrent voice still possible in the wake of military disaster; and could it still be found in the structural devices and the singular distribution of internal strength which were presented by the Democratic Party? An answer, the full import of which has perhaps never been fully recognized, began to emerge as the Southern states went back into Congress in the 1870s.

anomaly of a social minority which was not always numerically the smaller group, within a political minority which was forever striving to maintain its power in the government and its basic sectional objectives, despite its steadily diminishing proportion of the national population and its steadily shrinking proportion of membership in the Senate and the House of Representatives. Much of the literature of the history of the South revolves around these two themes—the history of the biracial system in slavery and in segregation, and the history of sectionalism.

It is the history of sectionalism which I am concerned with in these pages. Much of the historical study of the history of sectionalism has centered upon political concepts and theories which are now obsolete—the doctrine of state sovereignty, the doctrine of strict construction of the Constitution, the doctrine of nullification; and not enough, I would argue, has centered upon the actual political practices by which the South continued to exercise something like a concurrent voice in national affairs. In the last years before the Civil War, the South did this, as I tried to show earlier, by its control of the Democratic Party. It exercised control in the party convention by the two-thirds rule, and also in Congress by the workings of the caucus as an instrument for determining the organization and sometimes the procedure of the Senate and House, by the criterion of seniority as a means of selecting committee chairmen, and by the committee system itself as a means of deciding important public issues.

But although these devices had worked for a few years before the Civil War, the South had scarcely gone so far before the War as to accept a one-party system as its means of attaining a concurrent voice. It would have been a bold man indeed who could have predicted that these same arrangements could be revived, reinstituted, and further refined and perfected so that, for another sixty years, the South might retain something approaching equality in the national political power—although this picture of sectional equilibrium must be sharply qualified by the fact that there were two long periods, first for fourteen years under McKinley, Theodore Roosevelt, and Taft, and another for ten years under Harding, Coolidge, and Hoover, when the President and the majorities in both Houses of Congress were all Republicans. Also, for the fifty-eight years between 1875 and the New Deal, there were only two Democratic presidents, Cleveland and Wilson. But for twenty-six of these fifty-eight years, the Democrats controlled the presidency or the House of Representatives. Throughout this era it is a fact of capital importance that the Southern wing of the party in Congress was almost always larger than the Northern wing. This meant that the Southern wing could count on holding a majority in the party caucuses and, thus indirectly, control of whichever chamber the caucus

31

pertained to. The extreme dependence of the party upon its Southern wing is strikingly illustrated by the following fact. With the exception of 1912, when Woodrow Wilson carried many states outside the South because the Republican vote was divided between Taft and Theodore Roosevelt, 84.5 percent of the total electoral vote cast for all Democratic presidential candidates between 1896 and 1928 (Bryan in 1896, 1900, and 1908; Parker in 1904; Wilson in 1916; Cox in 1920; Davis in 1924; and Smith in 1928) was cast in the Southern and Border states. By the South, I mean the eleven states of the Confederacy. By the Border, I mean Maryland, West Virginia, Kentucky, Missouri, and Oklahoma.

When Lee surrendered at Appomattox, the prospects for maintaining power in the White South seemed remote indeed. Already outstripped in population before 1860, the South had fallen further by 1870 to 24 percent of the national population. After this the Southern proportion of population remained fairly constant. It was 25 percent in 1900, 23 percent in 1930, and 24 percent in 1960.

But for functional purposes, these figures are by no means the measure of the South's numerical vulnerability. It must be remembered that all of the Southern state governments which were organized by Presidents Lincoln and Johnson in 1865 and 1866 excluded Negroes from the suffrage. The Republicans were quick to perceive a great potential irony in a situation where Negroes, as free persons, would be counted fully for purposes of representation but would not vote. Before the Civil War, the South's slaves had been counted at a three-fifths ratio for purposes of representation, and Northerners had never ceased to complain of the unfairness of this arrangement. In fact Lincoln had made a point of it in the Lincoln-Douglas debates. Now, if the states reconstructed under Andrew Johnson were accepted on the basis on which he proposed to accept them, the South's freedmen would count at the rate of five-fifths for purposes of representation, although none of them would vote. Under the old ratio, the South had had eighteen extra seats because of its slave property, but now it would receive a bonus of twelve additional seats for its failure to prevent the emancipation of the slaves. In total the Southern region would enjoy the possession of thirty seats by virtue of a Negro population which was not permitted to vote. James A. Garfield of Ohio recognized this anomaly and stated it with heavy rhetorical emphasis on the floor of the House.

> Shall the death of slavery add two-fifths to the entire power which slavery had when slavery was living? Shall one white man have as much share in the government as three other white men merely because he lives where blacks outnumber whites two to one? Shall this inequality exist, and exist only in favor of those who without cause drenched the land with blood and

covered it with mourning? Shall such be the reward of those who did the foulest and guiltiest act which crimsons the annals of recorded time? No, sir; not if I can help it.

The Republicans in 1866, as determined as Garfield that the Southern Democrats should not gain by the emancipation of the slaves, included a clause in the Fourteenth Amendment providing that when the right of any twenty-one-year-old male to vote in an election of federal or state officials was denied by a state, for any reason except crime or participation in the rebellion, the basis of representation of that state should "be reduced in the proportion which the number of such male citizens shall bear to the whole number of male citizens twenty-one years of age in such state."

If the former slave states had ratified the Fourteenth Amendment at that time, the Johnson-sponsored governments would no doubt have been confronted with legislation which presented them with the unpleasant choice so clearly posed by the amendment—they must share political power with their Negro citizens or they must have their representation cut. If their representation had been cut, their minority position in the nation would have been even more pronounced and would in fact have rendered them politically impotent, especially in the House of Representatives, which was their stronghold between 1875 and 1932. For the white population of the South

34

ern states were sending Republicans to Congress. Neither Garfield nor any other Republican could see any reason to reduce the Southern basis of representation while this situation prevailed. Indeed there was none. But between 1870 and 1877, every one of the ten, still steeped in sin, threw off carpetbag rule. As they did so, they marched into the ranks of the Democratic Party, and simultaneously they began the gradual but ultimately total process of disfranchising their Negro citizens. At first, this process was not institutionalized. Instead it relied upon intimidation, pressure, and trickery, or dishonest devices such as the eight-box law in South Carolina and the use of the tissue-paper ballot. Also, at first disfranchisement was not complete, and Negroes continued to vote in large numbers and even to maintain the ascendancy in a few congressional districts, but not in any entire states—not even the states where they were numerically superior. Later, between 1890 and 1908, disfranchisement was formalized by elaborate constitutional and statutory devices which never spoke of Negroes directly but which struck at points where the Negro was vulnerable, such as his illiteracy, and which provided loopholes such as the grandfather clause and the understanding clause, by which whites who could not meet the regular qualifications could qualify on an alternative basis. Broad latitude was allowed to registrars of voters to exercise their own discretion in the application of these laws, which meant in fact to register whites but to refuse to register Negroes. Thus Negro disfranchisement was completed. Within two years after the disfranchisement in Louisiana, for instance, the Negro voter registration in the state fell from 130,300 to 5,300.

But the remarkable feature which historians have not remarked about all this, is that the South had adroitly escaped the dilemma of the Fourteenth Amendment. It had denied the suffrage to a very large number of males over twenty-one, including incidentally a great many of its impoverished and disadvantaged whites as well as virtually all of its Negroes, but it had not had its basis of representation reduced. Slavery dead, in the telling phrase of James A. Garfield, had gained more power than slavery living. The White South continued to enjoy the advantage of this overrepresentation—for almost three-quarters of a century—until Southern Negroes were again admitted at the polls in the 1960s.

As the Redeemer governments began sending Democrats to Congress, the Southern Democrats soon grew to outnumber the Northern Democrats in House and Senate. As early as 1875, 86 representatives from the former slave areas were among the 169 members who formed the Democratic majority in the Forty-fourth Congress. Not until 1881 were a majority of the Democratic members of the Senate from the South. But when this time came, it meant that the South could again control Democratic Party caucuses by sheer numerical superiority. As the few remaining carpetbaggers and Negro members came to the ends of their terms, they were replaced by Democrats and thus Southern control in the caucuses was reinforced. The South was now for the first time, as Calhoun had wished, a solid South, save for the period of Populist revolt, and for a handful of districts in the mountain coves of the Southern Appalachians, or in Black Belt districts along the Mississippi, or in the Carolina low country where the proportion of Negroes was overwhelming (even these latter ceased to be exceptions in the 1890s). But as Calhoun had not foreseen, the Solid South, with the aid of such Border states as Maryland, West Virginia, and Missouri, formed a majority almost constantly within the Democratic Party in both the Senate and the House for a period of fifty-eight years. The only exceptions were when tidal waves of Northern Democrats swept into the House in 1883–1887, 1891–1893, and 1913–1915 and then swept out again as abruptly as they had come.

During these six decades of Southern ascendancy within the party, the Southern leadership in Senate and House perfected those devices of obstruction and of strategic control which it had begun to develop before the Civil War. In the Senate, as I shall show later, the Southern Democrats began to exploit the possibilities of unlimited debate. In the House the Southern leadership encouraged the development of an extremely complex labyrinth of procedural intricacies. It became entirely impossible to accomplish anything on the floor of the House unless the Committee on Rules had approved a specified schedule of procedure indicating when a bill could be introduced, what kinds of amendments (if any) should be allowed, how much debate would be permitted, and who would control the allocation of this permitted time. In other words, power resided in the Committee on Rules, as much as in the House. Speaker Thomas B. Reed, a Republican from Maine, engaged in titanic and victorious struggles to curb the obstructionism of the Democrats. In a speech before the City Club of Chicago in 1908, Reed put his finger on the source of this reluctance of congressmen to give the Congress power to act. "Ever since the slavery question came to trouble the peace of the country," said Reed, "the rules of the House have been framed with the view of rendering legislation difficult. The South was anxious that there should be ample means at its disposal to stop any measure detrimental to its cherished institution." After slavery ended, the South was still sensitive to any "outside" intervention in its biracial system. Hence it remained desirous of "rendering legislation difficult." The Rules of the House adopted by the Democrats under Speaker Charles F. Crisp of Georgia reflected this desire, just as the Reed Rules, adopted by the Republicans when Reed was speaker, reflected a purpose to facilitate the execution of the majority purpose by limiting the opportunities for obstruction allowed to the minority.

While limiting the powers of action on the floor, Southern Democrats (the term soon became a tautology) in the Senate and the House also tended to exalt the powers of the caucus, where they almost always had a majority, as well as the powers of committees and committee chairmen, where the increasingly immutable rules of seniority gave them an advantage which they exploited skillfully.

Most discussions of the caucus in the American Congress, as David J. Rothman has observed, have suffered by too much comparison with the British system and by a consequent conclusion that the power of the caucus in the American system has been relatively negligible. There is, of course, a measure of truth in this, for the American senator or representative depends on his constituents and not on his party for reelection. The party knows this and knows that it will only destroy itself if it tries to force a congressman to vote against the wishes of his constituents. If the attempt to force him does not succeed, it may disrupt the party; and if it does succeed, it may weaken the party by causing a good party man to fail of reelection. Hence the parties have consistently been extremely chary of holding binding caucuses on any issues except those of organization. Especially have they avoided caucus commitment on important controversial issues. Yet the fact remains that countless questions have been threshed out in caucus, and countless informal decisions have been made which influenced the voting behavior of countless members. The frequent near-solidarity of party voting on innumerable roll calls, especially in the late nineteenth and early twentieth centuries, is testimony enough to this fact. But the proceedings of caucuses were usually secret, at least technically, although they were regularly reported with a good deal of accuracy in the newspapers, and the congressional caucuses have never been adequately researched by American political scientists. Hence the most conflicting views have been held: One senator— a Republican, I must admit—could say: "I have been here [in Washington] nearly twenty-four years and have attended every [party] conference when I have been in the city, and the Republican Party has never undertaken to bind its members to vote on any question whatever." Yet Senator James Z. George of Mississippi was told that "the decision of a Republican caucus is like the decree of an ecumenical council. . . . The decree is infallible and everybody is bound to obey or be anathematized." Rothman, who cites both of these quotations, shrewdly recognizes that there is a measure of truth in each. He says:

> The caucus "was not binding, and yet its decisions commanded obedience, for party leadership was capable of giving or withholding things which might be vital to the average member. Congressmen could not

ignore this party leadership without forfeiting their claims to desirable committee posts, to floor consideration for minor measures which no other member cared about but which might be very important to their districts, and to the host of small favors and accommodations which could help a Congressman immeasurably in steering a successful course. "Mr. Sam" Rayburn summarized it all in eleven words when he said, as he did say so often, "If you want to get along, you've got to go along."

All this is equivalent to saying that no congressional caucus can succeed if it tries to be much tighter than the natural coherence of the members who constitute it. But this factor has varied from time to time and from party to party. Despite occasional bitter quarrels such as that between Grover Cleveland and the free silverites, coherence was naturally high among the Democrats of the late nineteenth and early twentieth centuries. Accordingly they formalized the caucus and made it about as strong as it has ever been in American legislative history. In 1903, upon motion of Joseph Blackburn of Kentucky, the Senate Democratic caucus resolved that the vote of two-thirds of the members should compel the obedience of every member. Benjamin Tillman of South Carolina, speaking in the caucus, declared that "any man claiming to be a Democrat and refusing to bow to the will of a two-thirds majority should be drummed out of the party." As the Democrats began to move back toward power after their long period of exile during the ascendancies of McKinley and Theodore Roosevelt, they began to tighten their caucus organization in the House. In 1909 Champ Clark of Missouri became the floor leader for the Democrats. Under his guidance it is said that the Democrats adopted a new set of caucus rules and held many binding caucuses. Two years later the Democrats captured control of the House and Clark became Speaker. This control gave them a trial run for the full power which came to them with the election of Woodrow Wilson to the presidency. It is evident that much of the success of Wilson's New Freedom program resulted from the discipline and effectiveness of the party caucus in the period between his inauguration and the First World War. The caucus instructed Democratic committee chairmen not to report bills to the floor of the House until such bills had first been approved in caucus. Indeed sometimes the caucus framed a bill and in effect transmitted it to a committee to be reported to the House. On other occasions the Democratic members of a committee would form a committee caucus to frame a bill, leaving the Republican members with no voice in the proceedings and no function except to acquiesce in a *fait accompli*. Oscar W. Underwood of Alabama was the floor leader during this period. He and a group of predominantly Southern committee chairmen used the caucus system to put through the Underwood Tariff, the Federal Reserve Act, and

State Democrats outnumbered Northern and Western ones only in the proportion of about 6 to 5, the numbers in the highest quintile of seniority were 36 and 8 respectively. In 1903 in the House as a whole, South and Border held 123 seats to 56 for North and West, but again, in the highest quintile of seniority, the ratio was 32 to 4. In 1913 North and West actually outnumbered South and Border, 152 seats to 138, but South and Border had all but 6 of the 58 seats in the top quintile of seniority. A similar pattern was evident in 1923 and again in 1931, when the South had 46 percent of the Democratic members, but 78 percent of those who stood in the highest quintile. In 1893 the non-Southerner with highest seniority was outranked by only one Border State man; in 1903, by 13 Southerners and 1 Missourian; in 1913, by 16 Southerners and 3 Border State men; in 1923, by 6 Southerners; and in 1931, by only 2 Southerners. But at that time, the 21 senior Democrats included only 2 from the North and West, 2 from the Border states, and 17 from the South. In the Senate in 1893, the 8 Democrats with greatest seniority included 5 from the South, 1 from Missouri, and 2 from the North; in 1903, 4 of the 6 with greatest seniority were from the South, while another was from Missouri and 1 was from the West; in 1913 the 5 senior Democrats were all from the South; in 1923 the 7 senior Democrats were all from the South or the Border states of Oklahoma and Missouri; in 1931 the

It is generally recognized that the combination of a good start plus the accumulation of seniority has enabled Southerners to dominate the powerful committees, but it is still astonishing to see how inordinate this control has been. Between 1877 and 1963, the Democrats organized the House of Representatives 26 times. During these 26 Congresses, there were a few important committees, especially Education and Labor (formerly only Labor) and Foreign Affairs, which the South did not dominate. The former had a total of 13 Democratic chairmen, of whom only 2 were from the South, for a total of 6 Congresses; the latter had 16 Democratic chairmen, with only 4 from the South, for a total of 9 Congresses. But elsewhere the South's control ranged from strong to overwhelming. On the Committee on Banking, Northerners from Illinois, Ohio, and New York held the chairmanship for 1 Congress each; 2 Border State men from Missouri and Kentucky held it for 9 Congresses and part of a tenth; Southerners held it for 13 Congresses and part of a fourteenth. Appropriations had 9 chairmen: 4 Northern or Western members for 10 Congresses; Clarence Cannon of Missouri for 9; and 4 Southerners for the other 7. But the Judiciary Committee never did have a Northern chairman until Emmanuel Celler gained the senior position which made him chairman for 8 Congresses. Military Affairs never had a Southern chairman between Reconstruction and the end of the nine-

it should be added, much fewer, for the Senate remained a Republican stronghold and the Democrats were able to organize it only 5 times before the New Deal, although they have organized it 16 times since then. I am therefore getting somewhat ahead of my story in summarizing the sectional distribution of Democratic committee chairmanships in the Senate. But in order to complete this analysis all at one time, it may be noted that Southerners chaired the Judiciary Committee for only half of the Congresses in which the Democrats controlled the Senate. The 2 committees of Commerce and of Interstate Commerce, and the successor committee on Interstate and Foreign Commerce, between them had 13 Democratic chairmen, of whom only 7 were from the South. Education and Labor, with its successor committee, Labor and Public Welfare, had 10 chairmen—4 from the South. Judiciary had 8 Democratic chairmen, only 4 from the South or Border. But in other committees, the South played a more commanding role. Military Affairs and Naval Affairs, later merged into the Armed Services Committee, between them were chaired by Southerners for 21 Congresses, by a Marylander for 1, and by Northerners or Westerners for 11. All but 1 of the 6 Democratic chairmen of Banking and Currency—Robert Wagner, for 5 Congresses —came from the South or from Oklahoma. All but 1 of the 6 Democratic chairmen of Appropriations— Hayden, for 7 Congresses—came from Virginia, Ten-

50

nessee, Missouri, or West Virginia. Seven out of 10 chairmen of Foreign Relations, for 15 out of 21 Congresses came from the South or from Missouri. Finance had but 1 Northern Democratic chairman, for a single Congress, seventy-three years ago. Agriculture never had a Northern Democratic chairman. For 21 Congresses, all of its chairmen came from Virginia, South Carolina, Mississippi, Louisiana, or Oklahoma.

What does it mean to be a chairman of a committee? Woodrow Wilson answered this emphatically but abstractly in his *Congressional Government,* when he said: "I know not how better to describe our form of government in a single phrase than by calling it a government by the chairmen of the standing committees of Congress." But to be more explicit, a committee chairman has extraordinary power over legislation. At one time a committee could not meet at all unless the chairman called it, and even today he can delay meeting for substantial periods. To a great extent he can control what shall and what shall not be considered in committee. Once a bill is brought from his committee to the floor, the choice of who shall speak and all the tactics of management are entirely at his disposal. If the bill goes to conference with the other chamber, he is assured of a place on the conference committee.

Sometimes the control by the chairman has assumed proportions that are almost grotesque. George

W. Haynes tells, in his study of the Senate, of one "large and important" committee during the years 1929–1931, to which 254 bills were referred by the Senate. Of these, 11 were considered, 7 were reported; and all 7 of the bills which were reported had been introduced by the chairman. Few committees can show a record to equal this, but almost any committee is accurately described by a statement made by Representative Sidney Anderson of Minnesota: "Of course the chairman of a Committee can not report a bill without the consent of a majority of the committee, but under the unwritten and, I believe, the unbroken rule, no majority has ever reported a bill without the consent of the chairman: on the floor, the bill is absolutely in his hands.

"It is obvious that the power to say that legislation shall not be considered is the power to legislate. It is the negative power which lends real significance to these chairmanships."

Negative power is the power of obstruction, not the power of accomplishment. It would never have sufficed for a New Deal, a Square Deal, or a Great Society. But that kind of power, the power of veto, the power of the concurrent voice, was the power which ruling elements in the South sought for a century after the Civil War. Despite its numerical weakness, the traditional South found such power, when the Democrats were in the ascendancy, in the party system. For the Southern wing often controlled

more votes than it possessed, through its ownership
of a majority interest in the party, just as a corpora-
tion sometimes controls more assets than it pos-
sesses, through the ownership of the majority interest in a holding company. When the Democrats
controlled the House, and the Southern wing controlled the Democrats, God was in his heaven, and
the traditional interests of the South were secure.

But it must be remembered that for thirty-two
years between the end of reconstruction and the
New Deal, the Republicans controlled the presidency
and both houses of Congress. During these years
Democratic seniority counted for naught, all committee chairmanships were in the hands of the Republican opposition and the Democratic caucus was
powerless. What did the South do then? The answer,
in a sense, rounds out the pattern of effective negative power—the South used tactics of obstruction,
specifically the power of unlimited debate in the
Senate, which was the last resort of an outnumbered
minority.

The power of a small group or even an individual
to obstruct action in the Senate by what is called a
filibuster was derived historically not only from the
lack of any restriction upon debate, but also from a
constitutional provision which caused the second session of every Congress to convene in December and
to terminate in the following March. This practice
was ended by the Twentieth Amendment, adopted in

1933, but while the short session lasted, the provision for an automatic expiration date held the promise for obstructionists that they did not have to survive a marathon of indefinite duration, but had only to prevent action until March 4. In such situations they could always rely on the fact that in the last days of a session, the urgency of voting such measures as general appropriations bills would be so great that the majority who favored a measure would yield to the minority who opposed it, as the price that must be paid to induce the minority to cease its obstruction. Occasionally a senator in the last hours of a Congress would demand some wholly unwarranted appropriation for a project in his own state, and the majority would recognize that it had to yield to this legislative blackmail. Benjamin Tillman of South Carolina did this in 1903 and William Stone of Missouri did it in 1913.

Such obstructionist raids did not constitute real filibusters. The filibuster involved protracted delay for days or weeks, heroic vocal exertions by elderly senators on their feet and talking all night, and a rich arsenal of dilatory tactics. The filibuster was not distinctively Southern, and until the New Deal perhaps the foremost exponents of the filibuster were Robert M. La Follette, Sr. of Wisconsin, and other Western Republicans whom Senator George H. Moses later called "sons of the wild jackass."

Actually the South used the filibuster in an organized way only twice between 1877 and 1933. But these two occasions gave evidence that the veto essential to a concurrent voice was always available and that, in the words of Vice-President Charles M. Dawes, "the open filibuster seems at times to be engaged in only as a reminder to the majority of what the minority . . . can do to . . . legislation if they are not appeased by its modification."

When the South's first filibuster was executed in 1890, no senator had been successfully called to order for irrelevancy in debate since 1848, and in 1872 the Senate had sustained a ruling from the chair that no one could be called to order for irrelevancy. Theoretically there was a restriction that no senator could speak more than once in the same legislative day on the same measure, but since any amendment was regarded as a different measure, and an amendment could always be offered, the restriction was meaningless. Moreover, demands for a roll call to determine the presence of a quorum were in order at any time. Freedom of debate was in fact unlimited. This was the situation when on December 2, 1890, the Republicans, holding a narrow majority of two in the Senate, voted to take up a bill already passed by the House for the supervision of federal elections in the South. This was what would today be called a civil rights bill and was at that time called the Force Bill. The Democrats went at once into caucus and agreed to resist the measure at every point. The Republicans, in turn, determined to force the issue by holding all-night sessions and by adopting some form of cloture. But the difficulty with all-night sessions is that they punish the majority, which must maintain a quorum, more than the minority; and the trouble with cloture is that every senator knows that he may some day want to use the weapon of unlimited debate. With great drama and amidst immense wear and tear, the Democrats brought action to a standstill until January 5, when enough silver senators, who wanted to adopt a silver purchase bill, voted with them, enabling them to set the Force Bill aside by a vote of 34–29.

Nine days later the silver bill passed, and the Senate again took up the Force Bill, when the Vice-President broke a 33–33 tie by voting in the affirmative. When Democratic filibustering began again, Republican all-night sessions also resumed, and Senator Nelson W. Aldrich introduced a proposal for cloture. His effort failed and after legislative convulsions that lasted until January 26, the Senate voted 35–34 to take up another measure. The Force Bill was dead after thirty-three days of filibustering, and the Southern Democratic senators had demonstrated that when the South was sufficiently aroused, the concurrent voice was still in effect in the American government, even though the Republican Party controlled the presidency and both houses of Congress.

In 1917, after Senator La Follette and what Woodrow Wilson called a "little group of willful men" had filibustered successfully to prevent the adoption of Wilson's bill calling for the arming of merchant vessels, the Senate at last, in an atmosphere of wartime emergency, adopted, upon motion by Senator Thomas S. Martin of Virginia, its Rule XXII, which provided that sixteen senators might petition in writing for cloture and that two days after they had done so, the proposal should be put to a vote. If it were supported by two-thirds of the senators present and voting, each senator would thereafter be allowed only one hour to speak before a vote on the measure under consideration. This carried 76–3 and not one of the adverse votes came from the South or the Border. But when Vice-President Dawes called for stricter cloture rules in 1925, Southern senators opposed.

Rule XXII was a form of cloture, without a doubt. But a two-thirds vote was hard to arrange in a body which cherished the privileges of unlimited debate. For the next sixteen years, that is until the New Deal, cloture petitions were submitted only eleven times and cloture was voted only four times—not once upon any issue important distinctively to the South. But in 1922 the South launched its second and most fully institutionalized filibuster when on November 27, a Republican moved to take up the Dyer anti-lynching bill which had already been passed by the House. The South girded for action; but unlike other filibusterers, who frequently denied a deliberate purpose to practice obstruction, Southern senators made explicit their purpose and their conviction of right in resorting to this weapon. Underwood of Alabama, floor leader for the Democrats, denounced the bill as a "rape of the Constitution"; he said without evasion: "I think all men here know that under the rules of the Senate, when fifteen or twenty or twenty-five men say that you cannot pass a certain bill, it cannot be passed." Underwood added: "We are going to transact no more business here until we have an understanding about this bill." On December 4 the Republican majority recognized that he could and would make good his threat and they dropped the bill. No more proposals for legislation in connection with lynching came to the Senate until two years after the beginning of the New Deal.

As of 1933, for sixty years the South had been gaining the ends sought by Calhoun—a negative by the South upon action by the federal government, despite the South's minority status—by a means which Calhoun had rejected, that is by zealous, even fanatical adherence to one political party. For a period of fifty years, beginning in 1896, the states of the old Confederacy, now known as the Solid South, sent approximately 2,500 Democrats and 100 Republicans to Congress. In the last twenty-six of these years, 579 of the Democrats were unopposed by a candidate of any other party. With this solidarity the South made a cult of the Democratic Party. I am indebted to Mark Thomas Carleton, of the history department, Louisiana State University, for a quotation from Governor Murphy J. Foster of Louisiana which illustrates this cult. When campaigning for reelection, Foster said: "Because I have sinned, don't destroy the Democratic Party; strike down the sinner. If I have been recreant in my duty, strike me down, but for God's sake, don't destroy the Democratic Party." In the haze of the Southern memory, the Democratic Party was becoming indistinguishable from the Lost Cause, and equally sacred.

But at the same time that it was sacred, it was also considerably more functional. The South in the nation was in a minority. But in the Democratic Party, it was in the majority. In the first third of the century, the Democratic Party was pretty consistently a minority, which meant that the Southern wing formed a majority in a minority party. Yet this minority party had enough strategems and devices to maintain the political parity of the South, despite the fact that the region was increasingly heavily outnumbered. The position of a majority faction within a minority party was therefore a reasonably comfortable, stable, and secure position.

But what would become of the South if the minority party ever became a real majority party, and the Southern faction became a minority within the majority? No one worried about this question in the days of James M. Cox and John W. Davis, for it seemed the most unlikely thing in the world to happen. Yet in 1932 Franklin Roosevelt won by a landslide which began an era of large Democratic Party majorities lasting for the next third of a century. When Roosevelt was elected, Southern voters rejoiced that the party of Jeffersonian virtue had triumphed at last, and Southern congressmen shouted hosannas because the long dry spell—dry in more ways than one—was over. But they had scarcely tasted the first fruits of their triumph before they began to realize that the position of the minority faction in a majority party is, in many ways, more insecure and more precarious than their familiar, almost traditional position as a majority faction within a minority party.

3

Rearguard Actions on the Southern Retreat

*D*ESPITE the Southern cult of the Democratic Party, which for several decades required worship at the Democratic shrine and treated cooperation with the Republicans as a form of sacrilege, the Democratic Party has never been a homogeneous body, but has always been a coalition. From the time when Jefferson and Madison went on their famous "botanizing expedition" to New York in 1791, Southern Democrats and Northern Democrats have seldom had much real affinity. Jefferson and Burr hated each other more than they hated the Federalists. Stephen A. Douglas and the Southern Fire-eaters were poles apart. Grover Cleveland and William Jennings Bryan might well have agreed that there was no rational basis for both of them to be in the same party. The South could afford to cherish the party and to support it with solidarity in the late nineteenth and early twentieth centuries because in a sense, the South controlled it. The South dominated party counsels, and the party was the region's vehicle of political power—an imperfect and limited vehicle, in the minority most of the time, a poor thing, perhaps, but its own.

But even when Southern control was at flood tide, antagonisms within the party sometimes broke out. They seldom became acute in Congress, for there the Southern majority was firmly entrenched, besides which, members of the party bloc in Congress had a way of adjusting their differences quietly and privately. But in the party conventions, where Northern delegates were not outnumbered by those from the South, dissension occasionally burst out in bitter, raucous ways which foreshadowed the strife that might come if the Northern Democrats ever ceased to be dependent upon the South for the bulk of the party's support.

One example of this strife occurred in 1912, as the leading candidate, when the balloting for the presidential nomination began, was Champ Clark of Missouri. But the Bryan wing of the party distrusted, or professed to distrust, Clark's affiliations with Eastern capitalists, and only three states of the Solid South—Arkansas, Louisiana, and part of Tennessee —voted for him. By the tenth ballot, Clark gained a majority. But the Southern opposition held firm for ten more ballots while Clark maintained his majority. After that, Clark's strength slowly declined, and on the forty-sixth ballot, Woodrow Wilson, who had divided almost all of the Southern vote with Oscar Underwood of Alabama, was nominated. For the third time in the party's history, the South had used the two-thirds rule to block the nomination of a candidate after he gained a convention majority.

Again in 1924 the Democratic Party almost destroyed itself in the most agonizing party convention since the debacle at Charleston in 1860. Before the balloting began, the minority of the platform committee brought in a report condemning the Ku Klux Klan by name. This resolution failed by almost the closest vote in convention history—543$\frac{3}{20}$–542$\frac{7}{20}$. The South cast 34½ votes to condemn and 209 votes not to condemn. Following this, the balloting began with William G. McAdoo first and Alfred E. Smith second in a long list of candidates. On the first ballot, McAdoo, who was believed to have the support of the Klan, received 146 delegate votes from six Southern states. Smith received not one vote from the South. For more than eighty ballots, McAdoo continued to lead the poll, with Smith second. Ultimately McAdoo came within about 20 votes of a majority, but never approached the necessary two-thirds. By the eighty-seventh ballot, Smith took the lead, but he still had only a single vote from the South. On the one hundred third ballot, an exhausted convention gave to John W. Davis a nomination which had already been rendered worthless.

The moral of the 1924 convention was that the concurrent voice was indeed concurrent. If it gave the South a veto on the North, it also gave the North a veto on the South. Politically the party could not afford the deadly cost of these vetoes, and McAdoo's candidacy, which had been strong both in 1920 and 1924, was never revived again. But the supporters of Alfred E. Smith, the runner-up of 1924, came back in 1928 to try for the nomination once more. This time Smith had the backing of the Arkansas and Louisiana delegations, as well as eleven other scattered votes in the South, but the South as a whole still voted against him. On the first ballot it gave 203 votes to other candidates and 48 votes to Smith. Despite this opposition he received 724 votes, which was only 8 votes short of the required two-thirds. This was clearly too strong a showing to be resisted, and without waiting for another ballot, 125 additional delegates, including 32½ from the South shifted to Smith and he was easily nominated. On the final tally, he had 849 votes, including only 81 from the South. Without any votes at all from the South, Smith would still have been nominated. The two-thirds rule no longer constituted a sectional veto for the simple reason that the South no longer controlled one-third of the delegates. In fact one-third of the convention votes was 366, but the South fell more than 100 short of this figure with 252; and even with the addition of the five Border states, the total vote was exactly the 366 which constituted one-third of

the votes in the Convention. The Southern veto
would no longer be a veto unless it received some
support from the North.

But if a Democratic candidate did not need the
South to win a nomination, he still needed it to win
an election, as the sad fate of Alfred E. Smith quickly
revealed. In the contest of 1928, Smith received 50
percent more popular votes than any Democrat had
ever polled, and at the same time a smaller electoral
vote than any Democrat since Reconstruction. Five
Southern states broke away from the Democratic
Party—four of them for the first time since Reconstruction. A number of writers have blamed the South
for Smith's defeat, alleging that the Catholic question defeated him in the Methodist and Baptist strong-
holds of Dixie. But in fact six of the eleven states of
the Old Confederacy stood by the candidate of the
party, and he owed his smashing defeat to the fact
that Herbert Hoover carried thirty-five of the states
outside the South, while Smith carried only two,
Massachusetts and Rhode Island. Mississippi, Alabama, and other Deep South states, despite their
aversion, went down the line for Smith, but New
York and New Jersey did not.

The election of 1928 left many elements somewhat
disoriented. The Solid South had been broken at last,
as Virginia, North Carolina, Florida, and Texas for
the first time supported a Republican candidate, and
Tennessee repeated a defection which it had first

committed in 1920. Most of the states which had supported Smith for the nomination voted against him in the election, and most of those which voted for him in the election had opposed him for the nomination. But the one important thing, which no one could recognize at the time and which made the election of 1928 the end of an era, was that this was the last time, except in 1960, when a successful Democratic candidate would need any Southern electoral votes at all in order to be elected.

Between 1928 and 1932, the shock of the Great Depression tended to restore some of the shattered harmony within the Democratic Party, and when Franklin Roosevelt was elected in 1932, the South regarded his success as another victory for Dixie, comparable to its triumph in the election of Woodrow Wilson twenty years earlier. Like Wilson, who had been a native of Virginia but a resident of New Jersey, Roosevelt was also a part-time Southerner— a resident of New York with a home away from home at Warm Springs, Georgia. Like Wilson, Roosevelt was a favorite of the South before the nomination, and on the first ballot in 1932, he carried the full vote of every Southern state except Texas, which voted for Garner, and Virginia, which voted for Byrd. This overwhelming and steady Southern support had been essential to Roosevelt's gaining on the fourth ballot the two-thirds majority which was necessary to his nomination.

But unlike Wilson, Roosevelt won by such a sweeping national landslide that he did not in fact depend upon the South for victory. Indeed Roosevelt's electoral totals were so great in 1932, 1936, 1940, and 1944 that he could have lost every Southern state and still won the election. The same was true of Truman in 1948 and of Lyndon Johnson in 1964. Only Kennedy in 1960 had to carry some Southern states to win, and even he did not depend upon the South, as Wilson and Cleveland had, to make up for a majority against him outside the South. He won in the South by 81 electoral votes to 47, but he also won outside the South 222 to 187. In short, every Democratic winner from James Buchanan through Woodrow Wilson (except for Wilson in 1912) used Democratic electoral majorities in the South to offset Republican majorities outside the region; but every one of the seven Democratic presidential victories since 1932 has been accomplished by majorities outside the South as well as within it—and, with one exception, by majorities that made the Southern support unnecessary.

This was a great watershed in the history of the South's role in the political life of the nation, and it was evident in the Congress as well as in the presidency. In congressional elections from 1896 through 1930, the South and Border states together chose about two-thirds of all the Democrats elected. But in the seven Democratic Congresses between 1932 and

67

1946, the South and Border states elected fewer than half of all the Democratic members. Historically the South had passed from constituting a majority wing in a minority party to constituting a minority wing in a majority party. The moment this happened, the institutional basis for the century-old concurrent majority was broken, and the South was placed upon notice that its traditional tenure upon power had but a limited time to run. In a sense, therefore, the great political transformation of 1932 marks the end of the story with which this volume is concerned.

Still, it remains true that the institutional devices of the concurrent majority—the obstructionist potentialities of the Rules Committee in the House and of the filibuster in the Senate; of the two-thirds rule in the Democratic convention; and the seniority system, the caucus, and the autonomy of the committee chairmen in the Congress—all these devices had taken such deep roots and were, on the whole, protected so skillfully by the champions of the Southern position that the carefully constructed Southern mechanism did not fall apart all at once like the wonderful one-horse shay. Instead it was defended in a sequence of stubborn rearguard actions in which the veteran guardians of the traditional Southern position were defeated time after time, but kept up an opposition which left them still formidable, even after the running battle, or perhaps I should say campaign, had continued for thirty-five years. My story, therefore,

maintaining lower labor costs, which meant in effect, lower wages, in the South. Therefore Southern congressmen tended to oppose measures which established uniformity of wages or which encouraged unionization. Again, the South in the 1930s remained predominantly rural. Accordingly it was relatively negative toward housing programs which channeled federal funds into urban areas. But in a broader sense, the South's misgivings about social change derived in considerable measure from the fact that almost any kind of change might challenge the biracial system. Wage and hour laws were resisted partly because they might mean equal wages for Negroes and whites. Federal housing was resisted partly because it might mean integrated housing. Federal power in any form was suspect because it was an implicit threat to the power of the states, and the autonomy of the states had been the foundation stone of institutionalized segregation. As for measures for the specific protection of Negroes, whether it was legislation to penalize areas where lynchings occurred, legislation against the poll tax, legislation to support the Fair Employment Practices Commission or a commission on civil rights, or whether it was direct civil rights legislation of the kind which has been enacted in the past decade, the Southern congressmen were always overwhelmingly opposed.

In positing the general Southern opposition, it is important not to oversimplify or exaggerate. For instance, if Southern Democrats were more conservative than Northern Democrats, this was partly because in the South both conservatives and liberals were all Democrats, while in the North, liberals tended to be Democratic and conservatives tended to be Republican. Roosevelt and Truman, Kennedy and Johnson have met with as much resistance from the North and West as they have from the South, but only the Southern opposition has come from within their own party. Also, it is important, as the late V. O. Key showed and as James Patterson confirms, not to speak too glibly about a "coalition" between Republicans and Southern Democrats. Often majorities of the two voted on the same side of a question and sometimes, as I shall show, they had an understanding which may be called a coalition. But the fact was that those who tried to establish a definite *entente* found that they had a rough road to travel. Josiah Bailey of North Carolina attempted to develop a working team of Democrats and Republicans, but as soon as it was publicized in the press, all the participants denied any connection with it. Even Carter Glass of Virginia, who yielded to no man in his hatred of the New Deal, insisted upon his orthodoxy as a Democrat. "I am . . . intent," he said, "upon preserving my party regularity, which in Virginia is almost as desirable as preserving one's religious integrity."

Bearing these *caveats* in mind, however, it is realistic to recognize that the congressional Democrats in general and the Southern Democrats in particular felt alienated from Roosevelt. Partly it was a matter of his policies. Partly it was simply that he took counsel with Brains Trusters like Moley, Tugwell, or Hopkins, with "upstarts" like Corcoran and Cohen, and with non-Democrats like Harold Ickes, rather than with veteran leaders of the Democratic Party. Partly, it may be added, he showed a certain callousness and lack of decency in the way in which he called upon congressional leaders to go down the line in support of measures on which they had not been consulted. His plan to reconstitute the Supreme Court, as well as a number of other important measures, were sprung upon the congressional leaders completely without warning. In 1937 when the Democratic leaders were on the way back from the White House, after the conference at which Roosevelt had given them last-moment information about his plans to increase the size of the Court, Hatton W. Summers, chairman of the House Judiciary Committee, broke the silence of the downcast group by saying, "Boys, here's where I cash in." It is widely remembered that, after a titanic battle, Roosevelt's bill was defeated in the Senate, but it is somehow almost entirely forgotten that in the House he did not receive even the dignity of a defeat. The Court bill was never reported out by the Judiciary Committee.

The feeling of the Southern Democrats that they

were stepchildren in a new Democratic Party was accentuated immediately after the Court fight, when the death of Joseph T. Robinson made it necessary to choose a new Democratic floor leader for the Senate. The Democratic senators would almost certainly have chosen Pat Harrison of Mississippi, a member of the small inner group which had directed Democratic policy in the Senate. But Roosevelt intervened with a letter to Alben Barkley, which was publicized, and which made it clear that Barkley was Roosevelt's choice for the leadership. After a short but violent contest within the senatorial group, Barkley was chosen by a vote of 38–37, but there is every indication that the Southern senators voted overwhelmingly for Harrison, and Barkley was never accepted by the Democrats as their own leader in the way that Harrison might have been.

Some Southerners were still supporting the President's measures, or a portion of them, because "party regularity" was a part of the creed by which they lived. Joseph Robinson, in the Court fight, was such a man. But believers in this creed also believed in the responsibilities of the President, as a party leader, to his party followers. Party wheel-horses felt that Roosevelt was amorally oblivious to his side of the obligation. Perhaps no group in Congress has ever followed a President with more private resentment than was felt by those Southern Democrats who continued to give at least limited support to

Franklin Roosevelt. The breach was finally and irrevocably confirmed in 1938 when Roosevelt went into the states of Walter George of Georgia, Ellison Smith of South Carolina, and Millard Tydings of Maryland and sought to defeat them for reelection to the Senate. The fact that all three were triumphantly returned to office was proof that while Roosevelt was popular with the Southern public, that public shared their senators' distrust for social change and stood behind Southern Democratic resistance to important aspects of the New Deal.

By 1939, as Patterson has shown, Congress was in full revolt against the President and defeated several of his key measures. It voted to investigate the shortcomings of the National Labor Relations Board; and the House, by roll call vote, refused even to consider either a $3.8 billion appropriation for new public works or a federal housing bill.

Democrats voting against these three measures totaled in the first case 104, of whom 72 were Southern; in the second 47, of whom 21 were Southern; and in the third 54, of whom 36 were Southern.

After 1939 the unifying effects of the nation's drive toward victory in the Second World War prevented a further split, although it did little to heal the rift that had already developed. But when the war ended and Roosevelt was removed from the scene, Southern objections to the civil rights programs, as well as the welfare programs of Truman,

Kennedy, and Johnson, caused a spread of the warfare within the Democratic Party. In the party conventions of 1948, 1952, and 1956, when civil rights planks came up in the platforms, and when questions were raised about the obligation of delegates to support the party ticket, Northern and Southern blocs fought each other like opposing armies and the carnage, at times, was appalling. In 1948, as is well-known, four Southern states—Alabama, Mississippi, Louisiana, and South Carolina—bolted the Democratic Party to vote for a new party of States Rights Democrats, or Dixiecrats. Never thereafter did the South return entirely to the Democratic fold. In 1952 and 1956, Virginia, Florida, Tennessee, and Texas voted for Eisenhower, and in 1956 they were joined by Louisiana. In 1960 Texas and Louisiana returned to the Democratic ranks, although it is said that the Negro vote accomplished this result in Louisiana; but Virginia, Tennessee, and Florida again voted Republican, while Mississippi gave all of its electoral vote to Byrd of Virginia, and Alabama gave him a majority of its vote. In 1964 the Southern political situation reached its supreme irony when the Republican candidate carried five of the seven states of the original Confederacy, plus his own Arizona, and not one state which Lincoln had carried in 1860. In fact, with the exception of Arizona and of Louisiana in 1956, Goldwater won only in states which had never voted Republican since Reconstruc-

plaining in the sessions of the platform committee; but when Senator Bennett Champ Clark of Missouri, son of the man who had been defeated by the two-thirds rule in 1912, brought in a report providing for the repeal of the rule, it was adopted without a fight and with no negative votes recorded, although the dissent of a fair number of Southern rebels was clearly audible from the floor.

In yielding the two-thirds rule, the evidence up to the present is that the South did not give up anything of substance. Roosevelt in 1940 and 1944, Truman in 1948, and Johnson in 1964 had more than two-thirds on the first ballot, and Stevenson missed two-thirds by a whisker in 1956. In 1960 Kennedy had a majority on the first ballot, and the convention was clearly in no mood to yield to any minority obstruction by the South. Only in 1952 did any nominee lack a majority on the first ballot, and only then did the South get what it really wanted: it defeated Estes Kefauver and it helped to nominate Adlai Stevenson. But one further point worth noting is that from 1948 through 1960, the South only once secured the nomination of the man whom it supported on the first ballot (Stevenson in 1956). In 1948 the South gave no votes to Truman and 266 to Richard B. Russell. In 1952 it gave 237 to Russell and 6 to Stevenson. In 1960 it gave 9½ votes to John F. Kennedy and 281½ to Lyndon B. Johnson.

The South could no longer exercise power in the

national conventions because it was in a minority, and what is more, a minority with which the majority of delegates were thoroughly unsympathetic. For the same reason, the party caucus in the Senate and the House was no longer an effective device in the defensive strategy of Southern leaders. That fact had been demonstrated when the votes of liberal Democrats made Alben Barkley majority leader of the Senate in 1937, despite a pronounced Southern preference for Harrison of Mississippi.

But some of the time-honored weapons of congressional warfare were still useful. In the Senate the filibuster could still be used, if not to make big medicine for the Southern Democrats, at least to delay the inevitable, and sometimes to delay it substantially. Even before the New Deal, many Republicans wanted a more effective means of curbing debate in the Senate. In 1925 Vice-President Dawes assailed the Senate for failing to adopt rules which would permit the Senate to act when a majority wanted action. During the Hoover administration, Congress submitted to the states a constitutional amendment which would eliminate the short or ''lame duck'' session of Congress and thus would, it was widely believed, reduce the opportunity for successful filibustering. This amendment was ratified in February, 1933, but it failed to accomplish its purpose, at least in any immediate sense, for the next two sessions of Congress, despite their longer duration, ended in filibusters.

In 1947, 1948, and 1949, Republican senators introduced a series of resolutions to give the Senate power to act with less than a two-thirds majority. But these maneuvers ended, to the confusion and amazement of almost everyone, with a change in the rules which actually strengthened the filibuster: instead of sanctioning cloture by two-thirds of the Senators present and voting, the new rule required two-thirds of the entire membership of the Senate.

For nearly a decade, beginning in 1953, Senator Clinton Anderson was the most active opponent of the filibuster, and in 1953 he advanced a concept which must have spread consternation among Southern Democrats. He challenged the long-standing assumption that the Senate was a continuing body and argued that at the beginning of any new Congress, a simple majority of the Senate could adopt whatever rules it saw fit to adopt, without reference to previous rules. In due course Vice-President Nixon gave his support to Anderson's denial of the continuity of the Senate. If a simple majority had adopted this interpretation, the long-standing power of the minority to block action by prolonged debate would have come to an end, but in 1953 Anderson was defeated by a vote of 21–70, and in 1957 he was defeated again 38–55. In 1959 Lyndon Johnson moved into this situation with the skill and finesse which made him, at one time, famous in the nation as a political magician and famous in the South as a defender of the Southern position. He consented to give up the

was imposed in connection with the civil rights bill of 1964, by a vote of 71–29; again in connection with the Voting Rights Act of 1965, by a vote of 70–30; and again, after two unsuccessful attempts, it was applied in connection with the Civil Rights Act for open housing of 1968. In 1964 twenty-nine opponents of cloture included twenty-one senators from the South—every one, in fact, except Ralph Yarborough of Texas. In each of these situations, the Southern Democrats stood almost alone within the Democratic Party; in every case they fought the legislation hard; and in every case, after the legislation was adopted, its advocates have proclaimed a sweeping triumph and its adversaries have bemoaned a disaster.

It would of course be fallacious to discount these announcements of a new era too much. Certainly there has been a vast transformation in race relations since the New Deal. Certainly the Civil Rights Acts of 1957, of 1960, of 1964, of 1965, and of 1968 have contributed and will contribute to this basic change in American society. They have been especially important in bringing American Negroes to the polls, and this in turn may have far-reaching results. But in fact the progress of civil rights has owed more to executive action and to judicial decision than to Act of Congress; and the proclamations of jubilee which have followed each of the civil rights enactments have to some extent concealed how much their advocates had to concede in order to get them adopted at all. Most of them were not, by any means, what the militant liberals had originally proposed, and every one of them had elements of a negotiated settlement—a settlement negotiated because Southern congressmen still operated from a position of power. In 1957 the original bill provided that the attorney general might file civil suits for injunctions against any deprivation of civil rights; these injunctions would have been enforced by contempt of court proceedings which, like all questions of contempt, would have been tried without a jury. But Southern congressmen secured modifications which greatly curtailed the role of the attorney general and which provided for jury trial in a considerable range of cases.

In the 1960 act, sweeping changes were made at the insistence of the South. For instance, important provisions to establish a permanent commission on equal job opportunity and to provide technical assistance for schools which were in process of desegregation were dropped entirely. Further, the powers of proposed registrars of voters to act through the use of executive power, rather than through judicial process, were very much curtailed. The success of the Southerners was in fact so great that it could be argued that they had won a victory which they were too discreet to herald.

The Voting Rights Act of 1965 was one of three

in which cloture has been imposed, but it also emerged in a final form which made substantial concessions to Southern opposition. Originally it included a ban on the poll tax and a requirement that federal examiners might supervise voter registration in states where less than 50 percent of the voting-age residents were registered. But ultimately the poll tax provision was dropped, and an amendment by Senator Dirksen was added which exempted states as soon as they could prove that 60 percent of their population of voting age was registered. This, it was believed, would invite segregationist states to drive hard for the registration of white voters to attain 60 percent registration.

Perhaps the only two measures on which the Southern congressmen have been forced into something approaching unconditional defeat were the general Civil Rights Act of 1964 and the Civil Rights Act for Open Housing of 1968. In these two cases, it may be pertinent to recognize that the first represented, in part, a delayed reaction to the assassination of John F. Kennedy, and the second represented an immediate reaction to the assassination of Martin Luther King, Jr. In both of these legislative battles, cloture was imposed, and in both the Southern leaders failed to secure much modification of the original bill. The original bill in 1964 contained broad provisions to protect voting rights, to assure equality of public accommodations, to facilitate school desegregation, to extend the life of the Civil Rights Commission, and to penalize racial discrimination in employment. This bill had the memory of President Kennedy's assassination behind it and was managed with great skill and patience by Hubert Humphrey on the floor of the Senate. Senator Russell of Georgia, who was leading the opposition, might have secured substantial concessions, but he adopted a strategy based upon the expectation that he could prevent cloture. Once he was defeated on this, the Southerners were cornered and it was too late to negotiate.

The act of 1968 also was truly sweeping and it provided for an extension of open housing requirements, through a series of three steps, to about 80 percent of the nation's dwellings. Again, the failure of Southern leaders to gain concessions may be partly due to the fact that their strategy missed fire. In mid-March the House Rules Committee, under Southern control, refused to bring the bill to the floor of the House. Clearly they were playing for time, in the hope that Martin Luther King, in his effort to generate support for the bill by leading a march on Washington, would instead cause a reaction against it. They could hardly had anticipated of course that King would be killed on April 4. But five days after his death, the Rules Committee reversed itself, and six days after his death, the House passed the bill, which had already been passed by the Senate under cloture, and sent it to the President.

in 1949 the House adopted a "Twenty-one Day" rule, by which a committee chairman could call up a bill which had been favorably reported if the Rules Committee had not released it within twenty-one days. Eight measures, including an anti-poll tax bill, were brought to the floor under the rule, but it was repealed in 1951 after a bitter fight. The power of the Rules Committee was fully restored, and in fact grew even more commanding when "Judge" Howard Smith of Virginia, a superlative parliamentarian and an extraordinarily resourceful man, became chairman in 1955. Smith's power was unchallenged until 1961, when the liberal Democrats went on the offensive. First, they tried unsuccessfully to drop Representative William Colmer of Mississippi from the committee on the ground that in 1960 he had not supported the Kennedy ticket. Then they induced Speaker Rayburn to join in an attempt to break Smith's grip on the committee by adding two new Democrats and one Republican to the group. This proposal was fiercely contested for four weeks and then carried by the narrow margin of 217–212. The three members were added, and within five months two of the "Rayburn majority," both Catholics who were offended by the lack of support for parochial schools in Kennedy's aid-to-education bill, changed sides and voted with Smith to kill the President's bill in committee. Thus Smith continued to hold strategic power until 1966, when he retired and the chairmanship of the committee passed into Colmer's hands.

In the Congress in 1968, the relation of Southern Democrats to the national party is indeed anomalous. The Southerners gain some of their objectives by coalition with Republican conservatives, which is an utter perversion of the historic tactic of maintaining Southern power in the nation through Southern power in the party. Southern senators filibuster against the measures of their own party, and the Democratic majority uses cloture to coerce the Southern Democratic minority. The South retains control of the Rules Committee and of the standing committees, and the Northern Democrats leave this control undisturbed, but they use discharge petitions to bypass the Rules Committee and special votes to avoid obstruction by the standing committees. For instance the Senate Judiciary Committee, under Senator Ellender's chairmanship, has never voluntarily reported a civil rights bill to the Senate, but the majority has sometimes forced the committee to report, by instructing it to do so; has sometimes taken up a House bill; and has once moved to bring a bill directly to the floor without sending it to committee. When Senator Morse objected to this procedure, Hubert Humphrey retorted that between 1953 and 1963, 121 civil rights bills had been sent to the committee but that the only one ever reported was reported under mandatory instruction by the Senate.

The Democratic Party as a vehicle of entrenched power for the Southern minority has almost ceased to exist. But if the tune is ended, a certain melody

still lingers. Thirty-five years after they became a
minority within the Democratic Party, Southern
Democrats still chair the powerful committees on
Finance, Foreign Relations, Banking and Currency,
Armed Services, Judiciary, and Labor and Public
Welfare in the Senate, as well as Ways and Means,
Appropriations, Banking and Currency, Agriculture,
Armed Services, and the Committee on Rules in the
House. The sages in the party know that while this
strategic advantage exists, they can afford to let the
national conventions vote for platforms of which
they do not approve and to let Democratic Presidents
claim that administration-sponsored civil rights bills
are more sweeping than they really are. In 1952,
when angry North Carolina delegates to the national
convention were ready to bolt the party because of
an "insult to the South," old Senator Cameron Mor-
rison told them: "We've been Democrats too long
to let any hotheads drive us out of the party. . . .
We are probably going to get a terrible platform
plank on civil rights. But we've had planks we didn't
like before and our representatives and senators
have been able to beat them off in Congress. . . .
After all, so long as we can hold powerful places in
the Congress, the President can recommend all he
wants to, but he still can't get his bills through if
our fellows won't help him." Olin Johnston of South
Carolina was thinking in somewhat the same vein
eleven years later when he said to his constituents:
"The last strength of States Rights is vested in the

powers of your representatives in Washington whom
you have elected and re-elected and re-elected. Their
seniority is the source of your strength and power
in Washington.''

Perhaps Johnston was partly whistling in the
dark. Southern power in Washington, as the senator
certainly knew, is precarious at best, and even Southern commitment to the Democratic Party may soon
be gone with the wind. But the fact remains that for
a century in our national experience, the South exercised something very close to a concurrent majority.
Done by methods utterly different from those which
Calhoun envisioned, this concentration of strength
nevertheless met his specifications, which recognized
negative power as the essence of the concurrent majority ''in all its forms and under all names.''

Insofar as it is true that, for a century of our national history, power was seldom exercised by a
numerical majority without restraint, and that it
could usually be exercised only by the joint consent
of two separate concentrations of power, this truth
might be regarded as a matter of prime significance
not only for the history of the South but also for the
history of the nation. In this sense it would perhaps
not be pushing simplification too far to say that one
important way of understanding the period between
the middle of the nineteenth century and the middle
of the twentieth, is to recognize that, in one of its
aspects, it was the Century of the Concurrent Majority.